PowerKids Readers:

The Bilingual Library of the
United States of America™

INDIANA

VANESSA BROWN

TRADUCCIÓN AL ESPAÑOL: MARÍA CRISTINA BRUSCA

The Rosen Publishing Group's
PowerKids Press™ & **Editorial Buenas Letras**™
New York

Published in 2005 by The Rosen Publishing Group, Inc.
29 East 21st Street, New York, NY 10010

First Edition

Photo Credits: Cover © Andre Jenny/Imagestate; pp. 5, 25, 26, 30 (Capital) © Joseph Sohm/The Image Works; p. 7 © 2002 Geoatlas; pp. 9, 31 (Farming) © Joseph Sohm; ChromoSohm Inc./Corbis; pp. 11, 23 © AP/Wide World Photos; pp. 13, 31 (Mounds) © David Muench/Corbis; p. 15 Cincinnati Art Museum, Subscription Fund Purchase, photo by Tony Walsh; p. 17 Library of Congress, Prints and Photographs Division; p. 19 © Robin Jerstad/Reuters/Corbis; pp. 21, 30 (The Hoosier State) © Reuters/Corbis; p. 30 (Peony) © Peter Smithers/Corbis; p. 30 (Cardinal) © Gary W. Carter/Corbis; p. 30 (Tulip Tree) © Lee Snider/Photo Images/Corbis; p. 31 (Wright, Porter, Bird) © Bettmann/Corbis; p. 31 (Walker) Madam C.J. Walker Collection, Indiana Historical Society; p. 31 (Tharp) © Petre Buzoianu/Corbis; p. 31 (Letterman) © Corbis; p. 31 (Crossroad) © Brent Smith/Reuters/Corbis.

Library of Congress Cataloging-in-Publication Data

Brown, Vanessa, 1963–
Indiana / Vanessa Brown ; traducción al español, María Cristina Brusca.—1st ed.
p. cm. — (The bilingual library of the United States of America) Includes bibliographical references (p.) and index.
ISBN 1-4042-3079-3 (library binding)
1. Indiana–Juvenile literature. I. Title. II. Series.
F526.3.B76 2005
977.2—dc22

2005006099

Manufactured in the United States of America

Due to the changing nature of Internet links, Editorial Buenas Letras has developed an online list of Web sites related to the subject of this book. This site is updated regularly. Please use this link to access the list:

http://www.buenasletraslinks.com/ls/indiana

Contents

Contenido

Welcome to Indiana

Indiana's motto is the Crossroads of America. This is because Indiana is located near the center of the country. A crossroad is a central meeting place.

Bienvenidos a Indiana

El lema de Indiana es El Crucero de América. A Indiana se le llama así porque está situada cerca del centro del país. Un crucero es un lugar donde se encuentran los caminos.

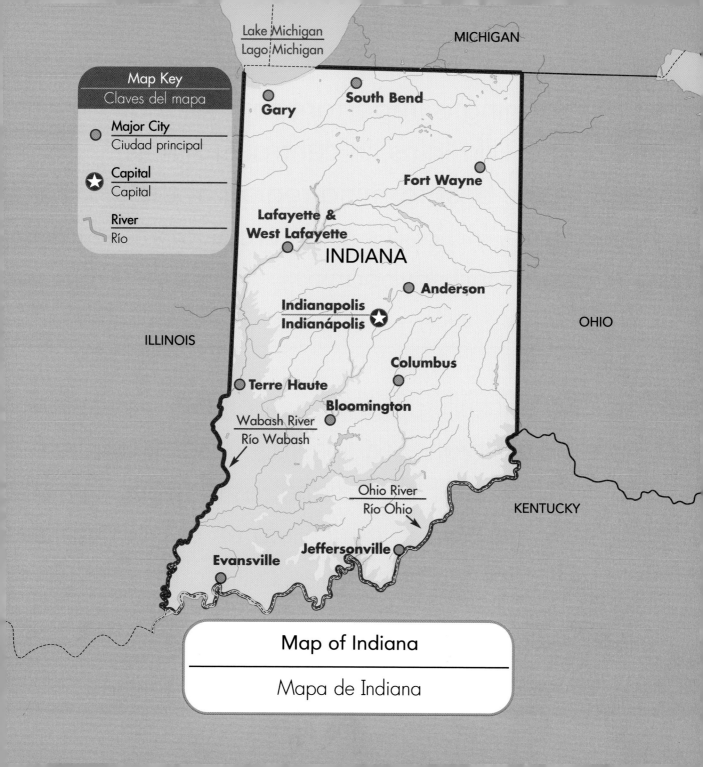

Lake Michigan
Lago Michigan

MICHIGAN

Gary

South Bend

Fort Wayne

Lafayette &
West Lafayette

INDIANA

Anderson

Indianapolis
Indianápolis

ILLINOIS

OHIO

Columbus

Terre Haute

Bloomington

Wabash River
Río Wabash

Ohio River
Río Ohio

KENTUCKY

Evansville

Jeffersonville

Map of Indiana

Mapa de Indiana

Farming is important for Indiana. The Till Plains, in central Indiana, is the best farming region of the state. Indiana's main crops are corn and soybeans.

La agricultura es muy importante para Indiana. La llanura Till, situada en el centro de Indiana, es la mejor región para la agricultura en el estado. Los principales cultivos de Indiana son el maíz y la soja.

An Indiana Farmer Working on a Hay Field

Granjero de Indiana trabajando en un cultivo de heno

The Wabash River is Indiana's state river. It is also the state's longest river, at 512 miles (824 km) long.

El río Wabash es el río oficial del estado de Indiana. Es también el río más largo del estado; tiene 512 millas (824 km) de largo.

The Wabash Cannonball Bridge over the Wabash River

Puente Wabash Cannonball sobre el río Wabash

Indiana History

Native American groups like the Adena and the Hopewell lived in Indiana around 500 b.c. These groups built large mounds. Many mounds can still be seen in Indiana today.

Historia de Indiana

Grupos de nativos americanos como los Adena y los Hopewell vivían en Indiana alrededor del año 500 a.C. Estos grupos construyeron grandes montículos. Todavía hoy pueden verse en Indiana muchos de estos montículos.

Hopewell Culture Mounds

Montículos de la cultura Hopewell

Levi Coffin was part of a secret group called the Underground Railroad. This group helped slaves escaping from the South to Canada during the Civil War (1861–1865). Coffin helped more than 2,000 slaves in Indiana.

Levi Coffin fue parte de un grupo secreto llamado el Ferrocarril Clandestino. Esta organización ayudó a los esclavos a escapar desde el sur hacia Canadá, durante la Guerra Civil (1861–1865). Coffin ayudó a escapar a más de 2,000 esclavos de Indiana.

Levi Coffin, Top with Hat, Helps Slaves Escape

Levi Coffin (arriba, con sombrero)
ayuda a los esclavos a escapar

Elwood Haynes was born in Portland, Indiana, in 1852. Haynes invented one of the first gas-powered cars. He also invented stainless steel, a type of steel that does not rust.

Elwood Haynes nació en Portland, Indiana, en 1852. Haynes inventó uno de los primeros autos que funcionaron a gasolina. También inventó el acero inoxidable.

First Car Made by Haynes in 1893

Primer auto fabricado por Haynes en 1893

Living in Indiana

One car race has made Indiana a world-famous place. The Indy 500, or Indianapolis 500, is a 500-mile (805 km) race. This race has been taking place since 1911.

La vida en Indiana

Indiana es famosa en el mundo por una carrera de automóviles. Las 500 Millas de Indianápolis es una carrera de 500 millas (805 km) de distancia. Esta carrera se celebra desde 1911.

The Indianapolis 500

Las 500 Millas de Indianápolis

Indiana calls itself the home of basketball. The Indiana University Hoosiers are one of Indiana's favorite college teams.

Indiana es conocido como el hogar del baloncesto. Uno de los equipos universitarios favoritos de Indiana son los *Hoosiers* de la Universidad de Indiana.

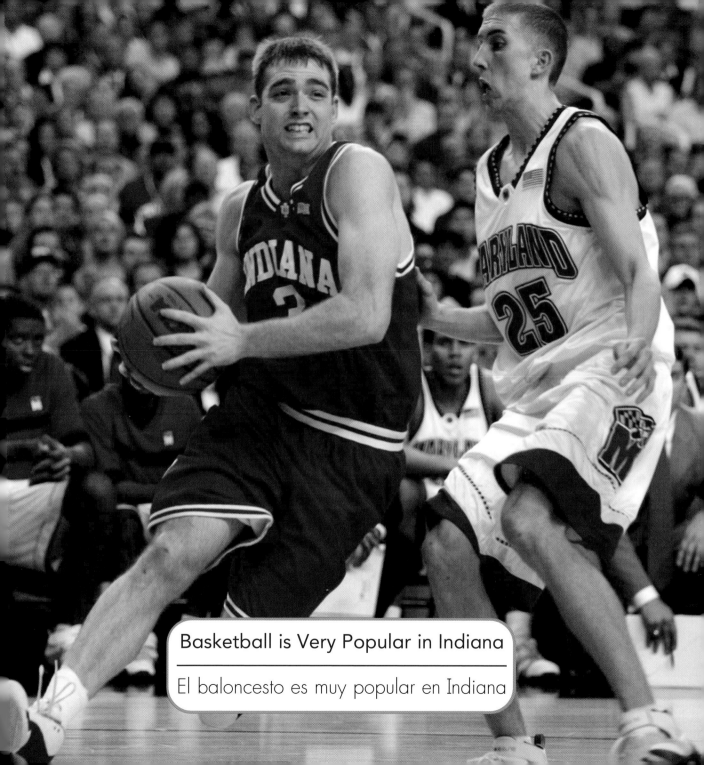

Basketball is Very Popular in Indiana

El baloncesto es muy popular en Indiana

Indiana Today

Indiana is ready for the future. Indiana produces many high-technology goods, such as aircraft engines, medical supplies, compact discs, cars, and medicines.

Indiana, hoy

Indiana está preparada para el futuro. Indiana fabrica muchos productos de alta tecnología, como motores de aviones, productos médicos, discos compactos y medicinas.

Automotive Plant Near Princeton, Indiana

Fábrica de automóviles, cerca de Princeton, Indiana

Indianapolis, Fort Wayne, Evansville, Gary, and South Bend are important cities in Indiana. Indianapolis is the capital of Indiana.

Indianápolis, Fort Wayne, Evansville, Gary y South Bend son ciudades importantes de Indiana. Indianápolis es la capital de Indiana.

State Capitol Building in Indianapolis, Indiana

Capitolio del estado en Indianápolis, Indiana

Activity:
Let's draw Indiana State Flag

Actividad:
Dibujemos la bandera del estado de Indiana

1

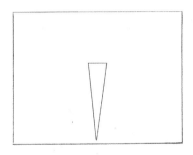

Draw a rectangle. Draw a triangle for the torch.

Dibuja un rectángulo. Traza un triángulo para dibujar la antorcha.

2

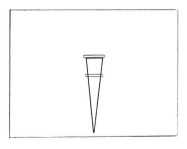

Add two thin rectangles to the torch.

Agrega dos rectángulos delgados.

26

3

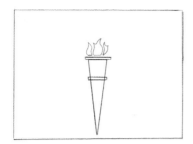

Draw in shapes for the flame as shown.

Dibuja formas para la llama, como en el ejemplo.

4

Add six lines coming off the flame. Erase lines in the upper part of the torch for detail.

Añade seis líneas a partir de la llama. Borra las líneas en las parte superior de la antorcha.

5

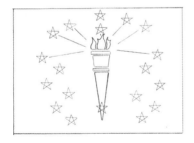

Draw 19 stars as shown.

Dibuja 19 estrellas, como en el ejemplo.

6

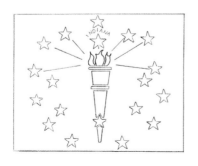

Erase extra lines. Write in the word "INDIANA."

Borra las líneas innecesarias. Escribe la palabra "INDIANA".

Timeline   Cronología

Timeline		Cronología
The first people arrive in Indiana.	**10,000 B.C./a.C.**	Llegan a Indiana los primeros pobladores.
René-Robert Cavalier de La Salle becomes the first European to arrive in Indiana.	**1679**	René-Robert Cavalier de La Salle es el primer europeo en llegar a Indiana.
The Indiana Territory is created.	**1800**	Se crea el Territorio de Indiana.
Indiana becomes the nineteenth state.	**1816**	Indiana se convierte en el estado diecinueve.
National roads are built across Indiana.	**1834**	Se construyen rutas nacionales a través de Indiana.
U.S. Steel Company builds steel plant and founds the city of Gary.	**1906**	La Compañía U.S. Steel construye una acería y funda la ciudad de Gary.
The Indianapolis 500 car race runs for the first time.	**1911**	Se corren por primera vez las 500 Millas de Indianápolis.
The Port of Indiana opens.	**1970**	Se inaugura el Puerto de Indiana.

Indiana Events

February
Park County Maple Fair in Rockville

March
Indiana High School Athletic Association Basketball Tournament in Indianapolis

April
Tulipfest in Bloomington

June
Bluegrass Music Festival in Beanblossom

August
Indiana State Fair in Indianapolis

September
Daviess County Turkey Trot Festival

October
Harvest Homecoming in New Albany

November
Indianapolis Chistmas Lighting Ceremony

December
Indiana Day , 11

Eventos en Indiana

Febrero
Feria del arce del Condado de Park, en Rockville

Marzo
Torneo de baloncesto de la Indiana High School Athletic Association, en Indianápolis

Abril
Festival del tulipán, en Bloomington

Junio
Festival de música bluegrass, en Beanblossom

Agosto
Feria del estado de Indiana, en Indianápolis

Septiembre
Festival Turkey Trot del Condado de Daviess

Octubre
Festival de la cosecha, en New Albany

Noviembre
Ceremonia de las luces de Navidad de Indianápolis

Diciembre
Día de Indiana, 11

Indiana Facts/Datos sobre Indiana

Population
6 million

Población
6 millones

Capital
Indianapolis

Capital
Indianápolis

State Motto
Crossroads of America

Lema del estado
Crucero de América

State Flower
Peony

Flor del estado
Peonía

State Bird
Cardinal

Ave del estado
Cardenal

State Nickname
The Hoosier State

Mote del estado
El Estado *Hoosier*

State Tree
Tulip Tree

Árbol del estado
Tulipero

State Song
"On the Banks of the
Wabash, Far Away"

Canción del estado
"Allá lejos, en las
orillas del Wabash"

Famous Hoosiers/Indianeses famosos

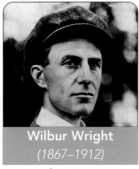

Wilbur Wright
(1867–1912)

Inventor

Inventor

Sarah Breedlove Walker *(1867–1919)*

Business woman

Empresaria

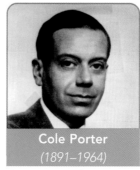

Cole Porter
(1891–1964)

Composer and songwriter

Compositor

Twyla Tharp
(1941–   )

Dancer and choreographer

Bailarina y coreógrafa

David Letterman
(1947–   )

Entertainer

Comediante

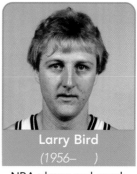

Larry Bird
(1956–   )

NBA player and coach

Jugador y entrenador
de la NBA

Words to Know/Palabras que debes saber

border
frontera

crossroad
crucero

farming
agricultura

mounds
montículos

Here are more books to read about Indiana:
Otros libros que puedes leer sobre Indiana:

In English/En inglés:

Indiana
By: Ling, Bettina
From Sea to Shining Sea
Scholastic, 2003

Indiana
By: Heinrichs, Ann
America the Beautiful
Children's Press, 2000

Words in English: 294

Palabras en español: 327

Index

Índice